Dinosaurs That Ate Plants

by Leonie Bennett

Consultant: Mitch Cronick

BEARPORT
PUBLISHING COMPANY, INC.
New York, New York

Credits

Corbis: Page 8; Dinosaur artwork courtesy of ticktock Media Ltd.

Library of Congress Cataloging-in-Publication Data

Bennett, Leonie.
   Dinosaurs that ate plants / by Leonie Bennett.
      p. cm. — (I love reading)
   Includes index.
   ISBN 1-59716-152-7 (library binding) — ISBN 1-59716-178-0 (pbk.)
   1. Dinosaurs — Juvenile literature. 2. Herbivores, Fossil — Juvenile literature. I. Title. II. Series.

   QE861.5.B453 2005
   567.9 — dc22

                              2005029869

For more information, write to Bearport Publishing Company, Inc., 101 Fifth Avenue, Suite 6R, New York, New York 10003. Printed in the United States of America in North Mankato, Minnesota.

022010
010810CG

10 9 8 7 6 5 4 3

The I Love Reading series was originally developed by Tick Tock Media.

CONTENTS

What did dinosaurs eat?

Some dinosaurs ate other animals.

These dinosaurs were **carnivores**.

Other dinosaurs ate plants.

These dinosaurs were **herbivores**.

What did plant-eaters look like?

Plant-eaters had small heads.

They had long necks.

Some plant-eaters had spikes or other **armor**.

They walked on four legs.

Some meat-eating dinosaurs wanted to eat plant-eaters.

The plant-eaters' armor **protected** them.

How big were plant-eaters?

Plant-eating dinosaurs were the biggest animals that ever lived on land.

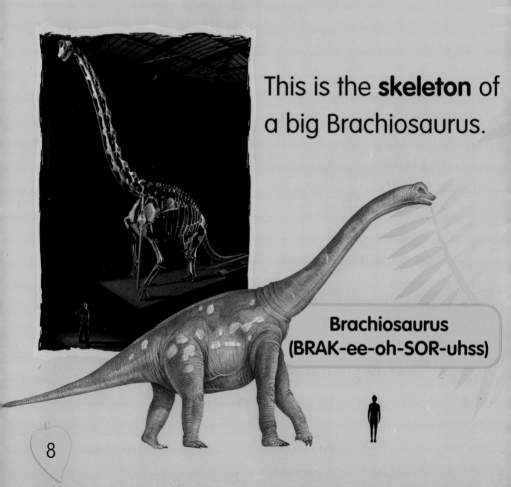

This is the **skeleton** of a big Brachiosaurus.

Brachiosaurus
(BRAK-ee-oh-SOR-uhss)

Seismosaurus is the biggest
plant-eater we know about.

**Seismosaurus
(SIZE-moh-SOR-uhss)**

How did plant-eaters get their food?

Some dinosaurs ate plants on the ground.

Other dinosaurs used their long
necks to reach the leaves on tall trees.

They did not chew their food.

They ate small stones to break up the
plants in their stomachs.

Diplodocus
(duh-PLOD-uh-kuhs)

Diplodocus had four big, strong legs.

It had a long tail.

Diplodocus needed lots of food.

It had to eat all the time.

Dinosaur Size

Diplodocus used its tail to hit enemies.

Stegosaurus
(STEG-uh-SOR-uhss)

Stegosaurus had lots of armor.

It had a very small brain.

Stegosaurus moved very slowly.

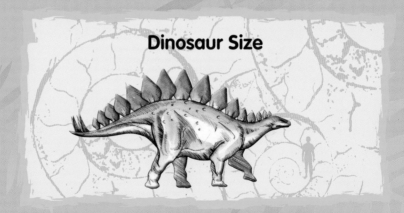

Dinosaur Size

It had **plates** on its back.

Triceratops
(trye-SER-uh-tops)

Triceratops had three horns on its face.

Dinosaur Size

It had a frill that was made of bone.

The frill protected its neck.

It used its beak to chop plants.

Frill

Beak

Euoplocephalus
(you-op-loh-SEF-ah-lus)

Euoplocephalus had lots of armor.

It had big spikes and plates.

Euoplocephalus had a club on the end of its tail.

It used its tail to hit enemies.

Club

Hadrosaurus
(HAD-roh-SOR-uhss)

Hadrosaurus could walk on two legs and on four legs.

Its mouth was like a duck's beak.

Hadrosaurus had a long stiff tail.

Dinosaur Size

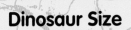

It had strong back legs.

Glossary

armor (AR-mur)
special bones that
protected dinosaurs

carnivores (KAR-nuh-*vorz*)
meat-eating animals

herbivores
(HUR-buh-*vorz*)
plant-eating animals

plates (PLAYTS)
flat pieces of bone
that cover the body

protected (proh-TEKT-id)
stopped something
from being hurt

skeleton
(SKEL-uh-tuhn)
the bones of
an animal

Index

Learn More

Zimmerman, Howard. *Dinosaurs! The Biggest, Baddest, Strangest, Fastest.* New York: Simon & Schuster Children (2000).

Zoehfeld, Kathleen Weidner. *Dinosaurs Big and Small.* New York: HarperCollins (2002).

www.enchantedlearning.com/subjects/dinosaurs/glossary/index.shtml

www.kbears.com/dinosaurs/index.html